# Fasting for Spiritual Breakthrough Study Guide

By

Elmer Towns

From Gospel Light
Ventura, California, U.S.A.

Gospel Light is a Christian publisher dedicated to serving the local church. We believe God's vision for Gospel Light is to provide church leaders with biblical, user-friendly materials that will help them evangelize, disciple and minister to children, youth and families.

We hope this Gospel Light resource will help you discover biblical truth for your own life and help you minister to adults. God bless you in your work.

*For a free catalog of resources from Gospel Light please contact your Christian supplier or call* 1-800-4-GOSPEL.

**PUBLISHING STAFF**
**William T. Greig,** Publisher
**Dr. Elmer L. Towns,** Senior Consulting Publisher
**Dr. Gary S. Greig,** Senior Consulting Editor
**Jill Honodel,** Editor
**Pam Weston,** Assistant Editor
**Kyle Duncan,** Associate Publisher
**Bayard Taylor, M.Div.,** Editor, Theological and Biblical Issues
**Debi Thayer,** Designer

ISBN 0-8307-1847-8

Printed in U.S.A.

# Contents

Is this not the fast that I have chosen:
To loose the bonds of wickedness,
To undo the heavy burdens,
To let the oppressed go free,
And that you break every yoke?

Is it not to share your bread with the hungry,
And that you bring to your house
the poor who are cast out;
When you see the naked, that you cover him,
And not hide yourself from your own flesh?

Then your light shall break forth
like the morning,
Your healing shall spring forth speedily,
And your righteousness shall go before you;
The glory of the Lord shall be your rear guard.

Isaiah 58:6-8

# INTRODUCTION

Across America and around the world, God is calling His people to the discipline of fasting. Christian leaders of various denominations have begun to use their influence to call their followers to fast and pray for a spiritual awakening in our land and revival in our churches. In various communities God has already begun to answer that prayer.

This study guide has been prepared to help you grow in the discipline of fasting. For some, fasting may be something new to their Christian life. Others may have fasted for years. In each case, these studies are designed to help you better understand as an individual or in a group setting the biblical principles of the fasts God has chosen.

This study guide is based on *Fasting for Spiritual Breakthrough* (Regal Books, 1996). You will need a copy of the book to fully benefit from the studies that follow. The study guide provides opportunities to think through the issues raised in the text and personally apply each of the nine biblical fasts in your own life. Reading the text and completing these studies will help you gain maximum benefit from the discipline of fasting in your life. Because journaling is a great tool for chronicling spiritual growth and especially helpful when fasting, you will find a page entitled "Notes" at the end of each chapter. This note page is for you to journal what you have learned about that fast, how God is speaking to you through that chapter, or other personal thoughts. The final chapter of this study guide—"Choosing the Fast God Chooses for You"—will guide you through the process of evaluating each fast and will help you determine which fast(s) need to be practiced on a regular basis in your life.

Many Christians still struggle with the need for fasting today. In the introduction to *Fasting for Spiritual Breakthrough,* I suggest nine reasons why the spiritual discipline of fasting is needed today:

- More than ever before, believers are in bondage to demonic powers and need strength to stand against sin.
- Believers throughout the world need solutions to the many complex problems and threatening situations they are facing.
- The Church is in desperate need of revival and every tribe, tongue and nation is in desperate need of evangelization.
- The world in general and the Church in particular are crying out for people of character and integrity—people who have found in Christ the emotional healing and strength to overcome sinful and destructive habits.
- The abundance of food has insulated North American believers from the realities of starvation and malnutrition in two-thirds of the world.
- The media has so captured the national attention that even believers are operating according to principles completely alien to God's will for their lives.
- Even with the abundance of food and medical technology in North America, people are not necessarily healthier.
- A great many believers have become so entangled in economic and social pursuits that they need to be set free to establish their testimonies and to influence others for Christ.
- Because of the growing influence of demonic forces and the waning influence of biblical Christianity in North America and the fact that believers need protection from the evil one.

Do any of these reasons speak to needs in your life, your church or your community? If so, God has chosen a discipline of fasting for you. I encourage you to find a prayer partner or become a part of a small group that will support you and hold you accountable as you begin fasting for spiritual breakthrough.

May God use this study guide to help you make a difference in your spiritual growth and in your world.

Elmer L. Towns
Lynchburg, Virginia

# Teaching Small Groups

The primary purpose of this study guide is to help you personally understand fasting and to help you grow as a Christian. But this study guide can also be a tool to help you prepare and teach small groups. A simple three-step process to successfully guiding small-group Bible study is a result of the following definition of teaching.

## Teaching is the preparation and guidance of learning activities.

Remember, talking is not teaching, and leading a small group is not lecturing to them about fasting. Also, listening is not learning, so your students may not be learning just because they are passively listening to you lecture.

**Step One: Preparation**
You begin teaching when you begin studying, and the way you study determines the way you teach. The questions in this study guide will help you dig into the Bible and the text *Fasting for Spiritual Breakthrough*. When the questions make you think, use them in a small group. The same question will challenge others as well.

**Step Two: Guidance**
Your role in a small group is to guide or lead discussion. Resist the temptation to lecture. Use the questions to give focus and direction for group

discussion. You are there as a resource person because you have previously answered the questions. You are a guide.

Compare your role to that of a fishing guide. The fishing guide walks or rides with you, guiding you to the best fishing hole. The guide knows the equipment, the bait and the best times to fish. The guide doesn't go along to catch fish but to help you catch fish. So in the small-group setting you are there to help others discuss, apply and learn how to fast.

**Step Three: Learning Experiences**

The questions in this study guide will help you learn and apply the lessons on fasting. So use the questions in your small group. In a classroom you might write out your questions on a chalkboard or prepare them on a transparency for an overhead projector. In an informal setting, you might have them written on index cards to share with the group, or you could prepare the questions and make photocopies to hand out to the group members.

Only use the questions that were meaningful to you as you went through the study guide on your own and that you think will be beneficial to the group. You can leave some out and add others that will help group discussion. Arrange the questions in the sequence that will best keep your group on track.

**A Final Word**

The focus of small-group discussion is not just good dialogue, arriving at deep conclusions, or even complete understanding of the topic. The purpose of Bible study is changed lives. Remember the final instructions of Jesus, "Teaching them to observe all things whatsoever I have commanded you" (Matthew 28:20, *KJV*).

I

# The Fasts God Chooses

For some, fasting is a form of political protest. Others view fasting as a means of purging the body and achieving good health. Some feature fasting in fund-raising efforts for humanitarian causes. And others call people to fast for revival in America. With so many voices saying so many different things, it is not surprising that confusion exists surrounding the discipline of fasting. Before looking at what each fast can do in your life, let's try to put this whole issue of fasting in perspective.

## God's Purpose for Fasting

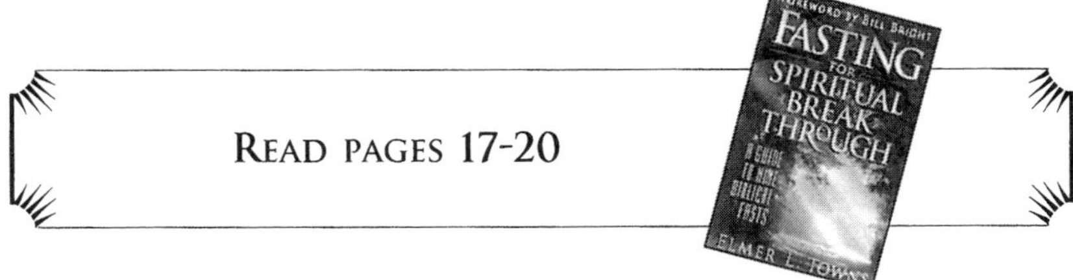


Chapter one begins with the statement, "From the beginning, people have pursued God." Examples are given of ways in which people wrongly pursue God. Sometimes even spiritual disciplines such as fasting can be practiced with the wrong motives and for the wrong reasons.

The Disciple's Fast is designed "to loose the bonds of wickedness" in your life (Isaiah 58:6). In what areas of your life do you have difficulty breaking free of bondage and/or addictions to sin?

The Ezra Fast is designed to "undo the heavy burdens" in your life (v. 6). Which problems in your life are significant enough for you to consider this approach to fasting?

The Samuel Fast is designed to bring liberty to the oppressed (see v. 6). If you were to fast for revival, what changes would you anticipate in your life?

What changes might you anticipate in your church?

Who might come to personal faith in Christ if you were to fast for their salvation?

The Elijah Fast is designed to "break every yoke" (v. 6) in your life. What is your greatest personal concern causing you mental and/or emotional anguish?

How might the Elijah Fast help you cope with this difficulty?

The Widow's Fast is designed as a means of meeting the humanitarian needs of others (see v. 7). What humanitarian needs are significant enough to motivate you to fast for them?

Is there a particular people group for whom you are most likely to fast?

The Saint Paul Fast is designed to help you gain insight in the process of making important decisions (see v. 8). What significant decisions do you anticipate facing in the next few months?

Which of these would be a worthy object of this fast?

The Daniel Fast is designed to improve your health and/or gain your healing (see v. 8). If you were to participate in the Daniel Fast, what changes would you need to make in your lifestyle?

What kinds of foods would be eliminated from or added to your diet?

The John the Baptist Fast is designed to enhance your testimony and influence for Jesus (see v. 8). How would you like others to think of you?

How could this fast help you establish that kind of character?

The Esther Fast is designed to protect you from the evil one (see v. 8). Is there a particular danger you are facing in your life?

Perhaps you have a particular burden for someone in a difficult situation or someone in a unique ministry situation. For whom would you be fasting if you used this fast?

## Four Kinds of Fasting and Physical Benefits of Fasting

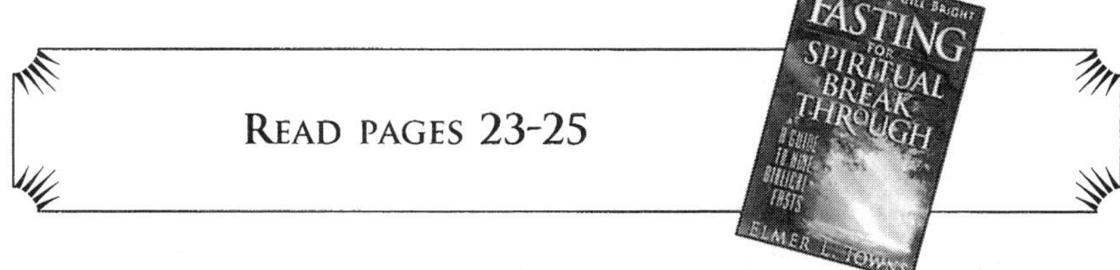


When God created us, He designed our bodies with a digestive system that uses food to provide needed energy to carry out various other functions. In North America, most of us eat more than we should and have accumulated stores of excess energy in the form of fat. In most cases, shorter fasts from one to three days will result in far more positive than negative effects in your life. However, it is always wise to consult your personal physician for medical advice about your situation. This is especially true for those considering longer fasts, expectant mothers, diabetics and others with a history of medical problems.

What medical condition in your life should be considered as you plan to practice the discipline of fasting?

In his book, *What the Bible Says About Healthy Living,* Dr. Rex Russell has identified four kinds of fasting as noted on pages 23-24 in *Fasting for Spiritual Breakthrough.* How would you describe these approaches to fasting?

Which approach do you feel most comfortable with?

Which of the many benefits mentioned by Dr. Russell would you like to realize in your own life?

## History of Fasting

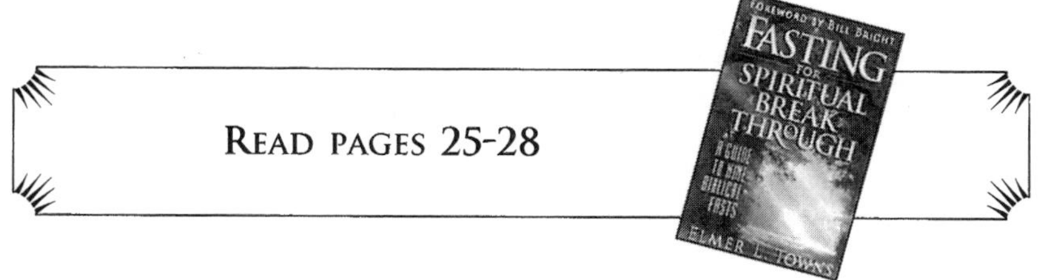


Few books have been written on fasting in the last hundred years. This might cause some to think of fasting as a comparatively new phenomenon.

How was fasting practiced in the Old Testament?

Based on the Old Testament practices, what are some times when you might fast today?

What did Jesus teach His disciples concerning fasting?

For what reasons did the New Testament Church practice fasting?

How did the Early Church practice the discipline of fasting?

What parts of their practices are you likely to incorporate into your personal discipline of fasting?

Throughout history, times of fasting and prayer have accompanied significant spiritual and political turning points in the life of a nation. What conditions in the Church today might motivate you to fast for revival?

What kind of political crisis in the world today might motivate you to fast?

## A Word of Prayer

> Heavenly Father,
> I have become comfortable in the abundance with which You have blessed me. In the security of my comfort zone, I have insulated myself from my problems and the problems of others around me. Now I sense You are calling me out of that comfort zone to deal with issues I have been avoiding. Lord, help me grow in this grace as I learn about and begin practicing the discipline of fasting in my life. In Jesus' name, I pray. Amen.

## Looking Ahead

Fasting is one of the disciplines God has established to achieve spiritual breakthroughs in our lives and the lives of others about whom we care deeply. In the weeks to come, you will learn how nine different biblical fasts can produce significant spiritual results in your life.

In the next chapter, the Disciple's Fast for freedom from bondage and addictions will be examined. Prepare for your study by asking God to show you areas in your life where you need to break free of spiritual bondage and enjoy the freedom that is yours in Christ.

# NOTES

2

# The Disciple's Fast

Sometimes it seems like everyone we meet has an addiction. Support groups exist for people addicted to both legal and illegal drugs, gambling, sex, food and even religion. While there are differences in each case and each kind of addiction, all addictions have at least one thing in common: Involvement in the addictive behavior develops to the point where the activity has a stranglehold on the addict.

Addictions may be as common among Christians as non-Christians. You may find yourself struggling with an addiction in your own life. While others think you have it together, there is something in your life that seems to be in control. One of God's chosen fasts, the Disciple's Fast, is designed to help break addictions.

## The Problem of "Besetting Sins"

The writer of Hebrews identifies the problem of besetting sins that many of us struggle with (see Hebrews 12:1). How are besetting sins defined (see pages 29-30)?

Does this describe some behavior or attitude with which you are struggling? In what ways?

What is the effect of a besetting sin in anyone's life?

How does Satan use these sins to keep us in spiritual bondage?

How can you break free from bondage and regain control of your life?

# THE POWER OF THE DISCIPLE'S FAST

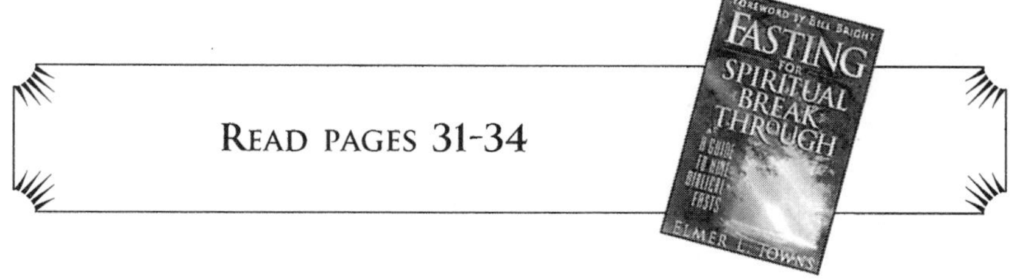


The Disciple's Fast begins with making a life-freeing choice to be delivered. Why does fasting strengthen our desire for deliverance from besetting sin?

Why must we recognize the external power responsible for our bondage?

How does fasting strengthen our faith?

Why is it important to identify in writing the bondage you want to break?

What about the person who fasted once and didn't experience freedom in Christ? Why didn't the Disciple's Fast work for him or her?

## The Prescription for Deliverance

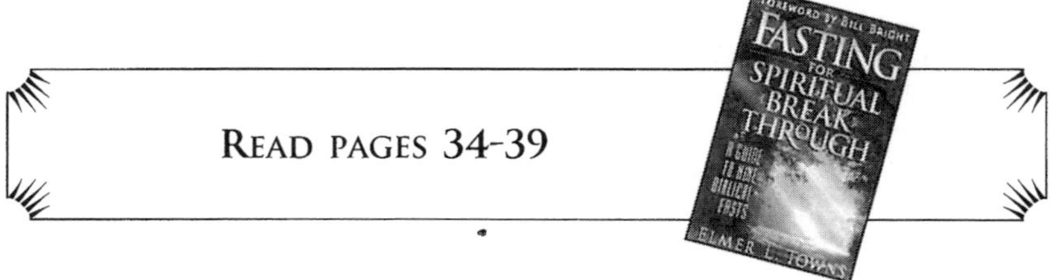


There are six steps in the process of breaking free from bondage as part of the Disciple's Fast. Let's look at these steps more closely.

**Step 1: Renounce Counterfeit Control**

How can you discern reality from that which is counterfeit?

**Step 2: Acknowledge Self-Deception**

How is it possible for us to deceive ourselves?

## Step 3: Forgive to Overcome Bitterness

What is the best way to overcome personal bitterness?

## Step 4: Submit to God's Authority

In what areas of your life do you struggle with authority?

## Step 5: Take Personal Responsibility

How does pride continue to enslave you to sin?

## Step 6: Disown Sinful Influences

How have you been predisposed to sinful behavior?

5. Take personal responsibility: I am responsible for...

6. Disown sinful influences: I disown...

Sin needs to be confessed only as publicly as it has been practiced. How public do you need to be in confessing your besetting sin?

## A Word of Prayer

Heavenly Father,
I find myself struggling with ____________________________
______________________________________________ and
am unable to overcome this problem on my own. My personal efforts to break free of this bondage have only resulted in frustration. Still, I believe You are able to accomplish far more than I could dream, even in this area of my life. Lord, as I follow Your leading in my life and observe the Disciple's Fast, guide me through the process You intend to use to enable me to experience liberty in Christ. Grant me the grace to be receptive to Your Word and submit to the principles You reveal there. In Jesus' name, I pray. Amen.

## Looking Ahead

Problems are one of the realities of the Christian life. In the next chapter, we will learn how to use the Ezra Fast for solving problems. Prepare for your study by asking God to help you take inventory of the problems you face in which the Ezra Fast could be part of your problem-solving strategy.

CHAPTER TWO

# NOTES

# 3

# The Ezra Fast

The only problem with the abundant Christian life *is* the problems. Sometimes we are tempted to think that our lives would be so much better without all the difficulties that come our way. When we try to blame all our troubles on our ultimate problem of sin, we recognize Adam and Eve faced their own unique challenges before the Fall. Problems are a part of life and learning how to resolve problems is part of the process of spiritual growth. In this chapter, we will examine the role of the Ezra Fast in helping resolve problems.

## The Problem with Problems

According to natural laws, everything that is made will break (see page 43). What are some of the things in your life subject to this law?

This part of the chapter describes three wrong attitudes toward problems:

- You are unusual
- You are unspiritual
- God has forsaken you.

When you face a significant problem in your life, with which of these attitudes do you struggle most?

Resolving problems begins with the right attitude. List the three problem-solving attitudes that will galvanize our thinking as we begin the problem-solving process.

1.

2.

3.

What was the problem facing Ezra that resulted in the Ezra Fast?

Is there a particular problem you are currently facing that the Ezra Fast might help you solve?

## The Prescription for the Ezra Fast

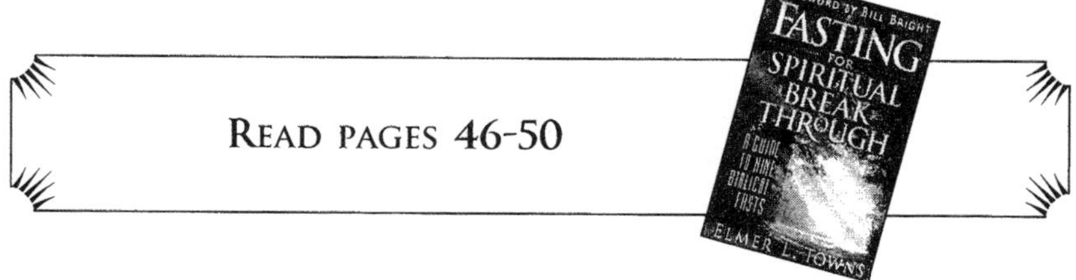


There are six steps in the process of solving problems through use of the Ezra Fast. As you work through these steps, begin by identifying a specific problem that will be the focus of your Ezra Fast.

**Step 1: Choose Those to Be Involved**

Are there others directly affected by this problem? Who should be enlisted to fast with you?

Why should others be interested in joining you on this fast?

**Step 2: Share the Problem**

How would you express the need in a way that might motivate others to fast?

**Step 3: Fast Seriously**

How serious are you about this problem?

How is this problem affecting you emotionally?

Do you share responsibility for this problem? Have you confessed any personal sin contributing to this problem? Are you actively praying for others involved in this problem?

## Step 4: Fast Before Attempting a Solution

Is the timing right to fast? How do you know the timing is right?

What is the spiritual aspect of this problem that fasting can address?

Have you attempted to solve the problem without fasting? Is the problem likely to solve itself whether you fast or not?

## Step 5: Fast On-Site with Insight

Is there a particular place that has special significance in relation to this problem? Would it be appropriate to visit that place to pray during the fast?

### Step 6: Fast for Step-by-Step Guidance

Are you willing to spend significant time considering possible solutions to the problem during the fast? Are there people you should meet with on the fast day to discuss the problem together?

## A New Perspective on Problems

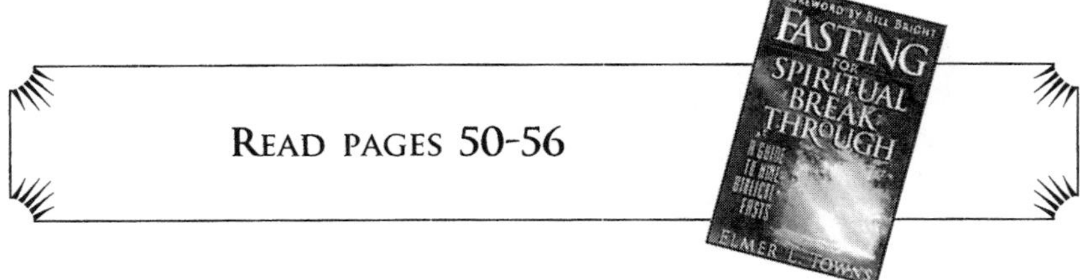


Sometimes, the way we approach our problems tends to magnify them rather than help solve them. The problem-solving Ezra Fast is not an attempt to escape problems, but to enlist the Holy Spirit's aid in tackling them. Use the following questions to gain a more complete perspective on the problem you are currently facing.

What is the apparent cause of the problem you are currently facing?

How big is this problem?

What are the basic issues to be addressed?

How can the problem be broken down into smaller difficulties to be solved one at a time?

Who is involved in this problem?

Is this a problem to be addressed or ignored?

What does the larger group think about this problem?

What good can come out of solving this problem?

Which people may be helpful in resolving this problem?

What do you need to know before beginning to solve this problem?

In what way can this problem help you to grow in your dependence on God?

## How to Solve Problems

This section describes a five-step problem-solving strategy that needs to be a part of the Ezra Fast. Use the following questions to walk you through that strategy as it applies to the problem about which you are most concerned.

**Step 1: Get the Facts**

Describe the problem in two or three sentences.

Is there anything missing from your understanding of this problem? What is it?

**Step 2: Establish Biblical Principles**

What biblical principles apply directly to this situation?

Are there additional principles which may apply indirectly?

**Step 3: Evaluate the Facts**

How has your view of the problem changed during your fast?

### Step 4: Determine the Various Solutions to the Problem

List several possible solutions to this problem.

### Step 5: Choose the Best Solution

Which solution is best in this situation at this time?

What steps should be taken to implement this solution?

## Practicing the Ezra Fast

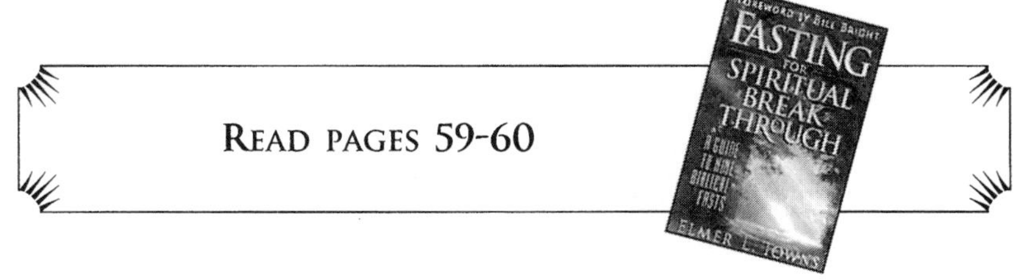


**Read pages 59-60**

As you prepare for the Ezra Fast, what specific problem are you hoping to resolve? Be as specific as possible in expressing your purpose in fasting.

What will be the character of this fast? From what foods are you abstaining?

When will you begin and end this fast? How often do you intend to repeat this fast?

Who, if anyone, will be fasting with you in this matter?

Will you be meeting together during the fast or fasting individually? How will you be holding one another accountable?

How will you respond if you do not have a solution at the end of your fast? Is there a commitment to continue the process of trying to resolve this problem through repeated fasts?

## A Word of Prayer

Heavenly Father,
The problem of ______________________________ has become an increasing source of concern to me. I am not certain how to best resolve this problem. But I know You have the insight I need in this matter and are willing to share that insight with me as I wait on You. Lord, as I follow Your leading in my life and observe the Ezra Fast, guide me through the process of problem solving to come up with a creative solution to this baffling situation. Give me the courage to carry out Your desires regarding the solution to this problem. Begin working in the lives of others so that a good solution may be implemented in a way in which You will be most honored. In Jesus' name, I pray. Amen.

## Looking Ahead

One of the greatest needs facing the Church today is that of spiritual renewal and power to accomplish the purposes God intended for the Church. Historically, times of prayer and fasting have played a significant role as the Church prepared for times of revival and spiritual awakening. You may sense a need for personal revival in your own life. In the next chapter, we will consider the Samuel Fast for revival. Prepare for your study by asking God to create a desire in your own life "so that times of refreshing may come from the presence of the Lord" (Acts 3:19).

# NOTES

# 4

# THE SAMUEL FAST

Not many took notice when Jeremiah Lanphier began advertising a noon prayer meeting in the North Dutch Reformed Church in Manhattan for September 23, 1857. Only six people attended. A week later, that number grew to fourteen. Within a month, people decided to meet for prayer every day. By February 1858, every church and public building in downtown New York was filled at noon as businesspeople gathered together to pray. A spiritual awakening had begun that would eventually reach around the world.

Matthew Henry once wrote, "When God intends great mercy for His people, He first of all sets them praying." Times of fasting and prayer have always preceded great revival. As we study the Samuel Fast together in this chapter, we will take a closer look at the unique relationship between fasting and revival.

CHAPTER FOUR

# Fasting and Revival

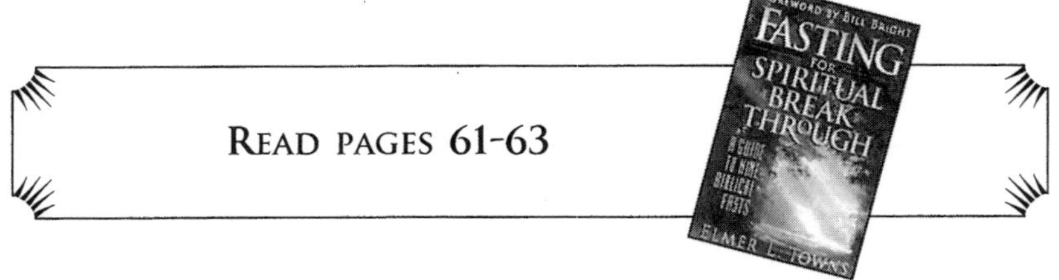


What were the three distinguishing marks of the great revival of 1859?

Atmospheric Revival is described as "corporate revival...when people feel the presence of God" (page 62). How would your life be different if the feeling of God's presence were more common in your Christian experience?

How does the expression "that times of refreshing may come from the presence of the Lord" describe revival?

What role did the Samuel Fast have in the national revival in Israel?

## Preparing to Fast for Revival

Before revival comes, we must recognize the source of our bondage to sin that hinders revival.

Why do you sense a need for revival in your life?

What do you see in your church and community that suggests the need for revival?

How would a sense of God's presence in your church and community make things different?

Who shares your sense of a need for revival in your community?

When is the best time you could meet with this group to pray?

Are you willing to assume leadership in praying for revival in your community? Is there another leader in your community for whom you should be more faithfully praying?

## Conducting the Samuel Fast

The six steps involved in conducting the Samuel Fast are common to any type of revival whether for your family, church or community. As you fast for a spiritual awakening in your personal sphere of influence, use the questions to guide you through these steps.

**Step 1: Call the Body Together**

Whom should you invite to join you in fasting and prayer for revival?

**Step 2: Demonstrate True Repentance**

What sins do you need to deal with in your life to demonstrate your sincerity in praying for revival?

**Step 3: Separate from Secret Sin**

What hidden sins has God revealed to you during your fast?

**Step 4: Have Corporate Confession of Sin**

What corporate sins need to be confessed by your prayer group?

**Step 5: Acknowledge the Power of the Word**

During your fast, read the scriptural accounts of great revivals listed on pages 70-72. What is God saying to you through these revival experiences recorded in Scripture?

### Step 6: Get in Touch with the Symbolic

Are you using the Samuel Fast as a legalistic tool to force God to send revival, or as an expression of your personal brokenness before God?

## AFTER THE SAMUEL FAST

How is Satan likely to respond to your involvement in the Samuel Fast?

How are relationships involved in fasting for revival?

What actions would God have you take in response to insights gained during the Samuel Fast?

What signs are there that God has begun to work in a unique way in your life, family, church and community?

What special answers to prayer have you experienced through this fast that will encourage you to remain faithful in prayer in the days to come?

## Practicing the Samuel Fast

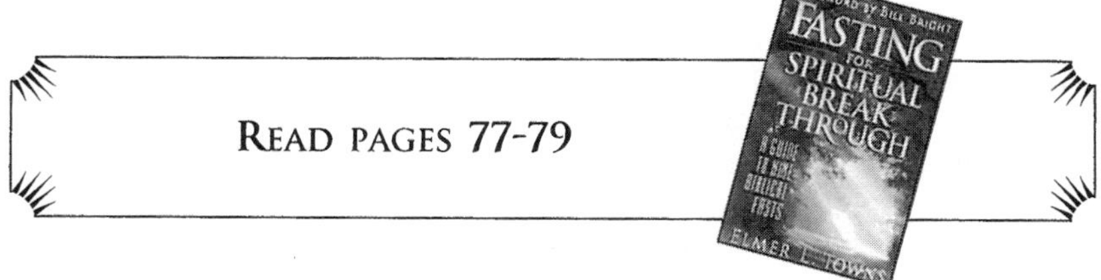


Why do you think the time has come to fast for revival?

Describe the conditions in your own life that motivate you to fast the Samuel Fast.

What concerns in your church cause you to think revival is needed?

As you begin fasting, what will be the character of this fast? From what foods are you abstaining?

When will you begin and end this fast? How often do you intend to repeat this fast?

The Samuel Fast sometimes dictates that you not pray for revival, but for God's *instrument* of revival—a godly leader through whom God can work (page 77). Who are the godly leaders God can use to bring revival in your community?

In addition to prayer, what other actions is God leading you to take to insure the coming of revival to your community?

There are many groups whose desire for revival is expressed in urging others to become involved in a significant fast for revival. The most credible of these groups are quick to urge Christians to begin with shorter fasts before engaging in a longer fast. Look over your fasting plans. Are you attempting too much? Would you be better off engaging in a series of short fasts than in one long fast?

Have you asked God to guide you as to the nature and duration of your fast for revival?

## A Word of Prayer

Heavenly Father,
In my own life, I sense a deep hunger and thirst for a deeper relationship with You. I am personally frustrated with my own spiritual impotence, and I long to see You work in a significant way in my life, my church and my community. I believe You want to revive Your people so that a significant harvest of souls might be gathered in these days. Lord, as I follow Your leading in my life and observe the Samuel Fast, reveal things in my life which hinder my relationship with You and prevent You from working in and through my life. Grant me the grace to be receptive to Your Word and submit to Your will for me as You make it known. In Jesus' name, I pray. Amen.

## Looking Ahead

People are creatures of habit. Some of our habits are good and commendable. Other habits are ongoing sources of embarrassment and frustration. Our inability to break bad habits causes us a great deal of irritation. In the next chapter, we will consider the Elijah Fast as a means for breaking negative mental and emotional habits. Prepare for your study by asking God to help you identify a specific habit in your life that the time has come for you to break.

# NOTES

# 5

# THE ELIJAH FAST

Why is it that bad habits are so easy to establish, yet so difficult to erase? As creatures of habit, we tend to do the same things over and over, even when we know they are wrong and say we want to stop. We struggle week after week, month after month, desperately trying to break a bad habit, but having little or no success.

The Elijah Fast is a fast to break negative mental and emotional habits. In this chapter we will learn about habits, how they are formed and how the Elijah Fast can help us break free of bad habits. As you work through this study, ask God to help you break a particularly negative habit as you observe your own Elijah Fast.

## RECOGNIZING THE HABITS OF THE HEART

While God used Elijah in a significant way on Mount Carmel, Elijah himself had an emotional problem. How did that problem manifest

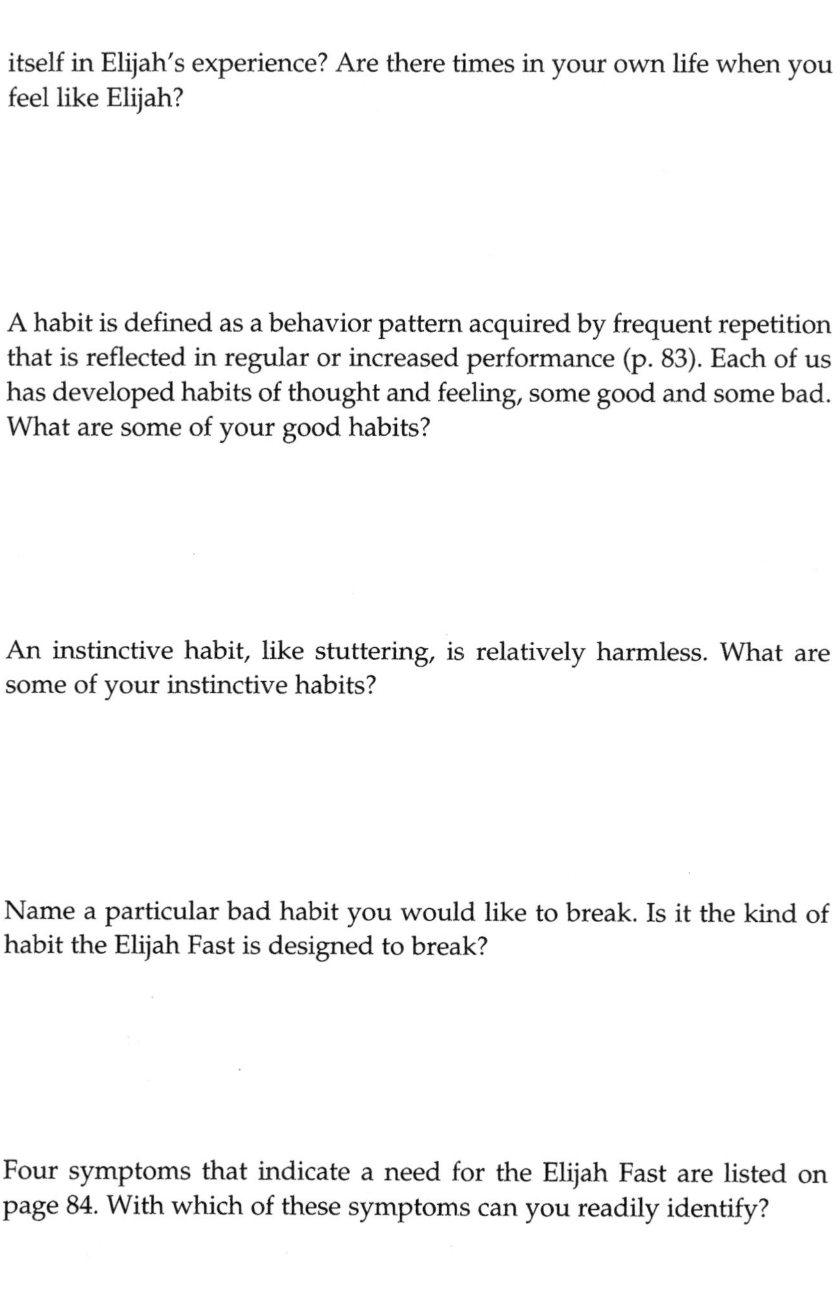

itself in Elijah's experience? Are there times in your own life when you feel like Elijah?

A habit is defined as a behavior pattern acquired by frequent repetition that is reflected in regular or increased performance (p. 83). Each of us has developed habits of thought and feeling, some good and some bad. What are some of your good habits?

An instinctive habit, like stuttering, is relatively harmless. What are some of your instinctive habits?

Name a particular bad habit you would like to break. Is it the kind of habit the Elijah Fast is designed to break?

Four symptoms that indicate a need for the Elijah Fast are listed on page 84. With which of these symptoms can you readily identify?

## LEARNING FROM A MAN OF LIKE PASSION

We are sometimes tempted to think of men like Elijah as super saints who lived near to God, with results far above anything we could ever attain in our Christian walk. But the New Testament describes Elijah as "a man with a nature like ours" (James 5:17).

Describe a time in your life when you faced a personal struggle during a time when others may have thought you were celebrating a personal victory.

We work hard at hiding our inner pain from others, but we cannot hide what is in our heart from God. If God were to take an inventory of your heart, what are some of the things He would find there that you would hope He would overlook?

Involvement in ministry is often a source of significant joy in the life of a believer. So we are surprised when we find ourselves discouraged or depressed while doing God's work. In what area of Christian service are you most easily discouraged? Why do you think you experience depression rather than joy in that ministry?

What past victories do you find yourself relying on to qualify you for future ministry involvement?

Based on your responses so far, would you consider yourself a candidate for the Elijah Fast?

## Prescription for the Elijah Fast

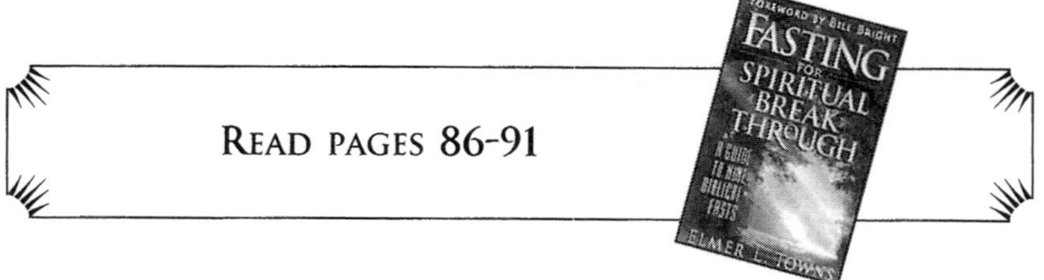


The following questions examine the 10 steps of the Elijah Fast:

What must you do to prepare physically, mentally and emotionally for the fast?

What limitations are you facing as you begin your fast?

Where do you need to go physically and mentally during this fast?

What Scriptures will you study during this fast?

As you study these Scriptures, what do they reveal about your personal walk with God?

What weaknesses do you need to confess to God?

How is God trying to communicate with you?

What is God doing in you and around you?

What positive steps do you need to take next?

What new thing do you think God wants to do in your life?

# How Habits Evolve

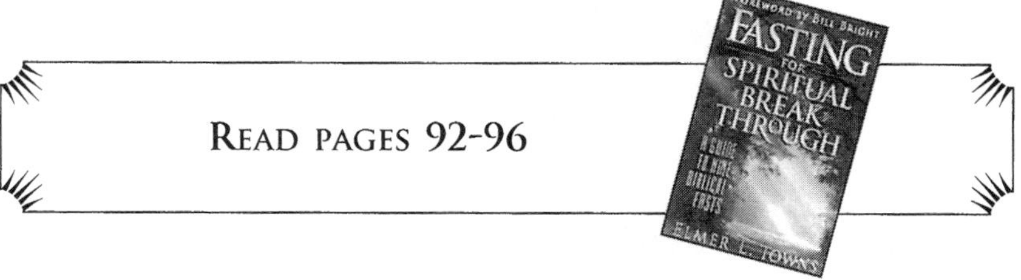


**Read pages 92-96**

Read the paraphrase of 2 Peter 1:4-8 on page 92 in the text. Based on this passage, there are six steps involved in the process of breaking old habits and developing new habits. The following questions will help you apply these principles to the habit you want to break.

How can you change your thinking to help you break your habit?

Which of the six responses to vision (see page 94) best describes your typical response?

What steps can you take to grasp God's vision for your life?

What steps do you need to take to change your attitude toward your habit?

What are some specific actions you can take to break this habit?

What good habit would you like to see take the place of your bad habit?

## Practicing the Elijah Fast

What habit do you hope to make or break through the Elijah Fast? Be as specific as possible when expressing your purpose for fasting.

As you begin fasting, what will be the character of this fast? From what foods are you abstaining?

When will you begin and end this fast? How often do you intend to repeat this fast?

Where will this fast occur? Is there a place where you can be separated from other influences during the fast?

What Scriptures do you intend to study during the fast?

Who will be praying with you during this fast?

What specific request will be the focus of your prayer?

## A Word of Prayer

Heavenly Father,
Despite past efforts, I confess I have been unable to break free of the habit of ______________________________ on my own. This habit seems to have a hold on me that is stronger than my will. But You are able to do exceedingly, abundantly above all I can ask or think to ask. I am reminded that You are my Helper in time of need. I need You and Your help to break this habit. Lord, as I follow Your leading in my life and observe the Elijah Fast, guide me through the process by which You will help me overcome this habit. Enable me to accomplish the things You want me to do, and help me trust You to do the things only You can do. In Jesus' name, I pray. Amen.

## Looking Ahead

People in need seem to be everywhere. We hear stories of victims of famine, war and disease. The world's problems sometimes overwhelm us, and we wonder if there is anything anyone can do to make a difference. In the next chapter, we will consider the Widow's Fast for meeting humanitarian needs. As you anticipate your study, ask God to show you how you can be one of His tools for helping the poor and needy in our world today.

# Notes

## 6

# THE WIDOW'S FAST

Jesus taught His disciples, "You have the poor with you always, and whenever you wish you may do them good" (Mark 14:7). That has certainly proved true today. Wherever we look, we find people in need. The hungry and homeless are under our bridges, on our streets and beyond our borders. It seems there are always more people in need than resources to meet that need. Still, as Christians we have a deep desire to meet the needs of the poor and defenseless.

One of the practical benefits of fasting is that it frees up resources that can be used to help others. This is one of God's purposes for fasting. Ironically, the Widow's Fast is named in honor of one who had personal physical needs but was willing to fast to meet the physical need of another. Because of her obedience, God intervened to meet both needs.

## FASTING TO MEET PHYSICAL NEEDS

Throughout Scripture, there are repeated accounts of people who gave, not out of abundance, but rather out of their need. What were some of the needs of the Widow of Zarephath?

What were Elijah's needs that the Widow of Zarephath could meet?

The Widow's Fast enables us to see God meet the needs of others, especially humanitarian needs such as food and clothing. Who do you know that could use help providing food and clothing for their family (e.g., single parents, the unemployed, disabled, elderly, etc.)?

Is there a larger humanitarian need about which you are particularly concerned?

While you may not be able to meet the need entirely by yourself, using the food money you save during your fast will address part of the problem. How much money would you typically spend on food daily? What part of the need could be met with the money saved during the fast?

# A Long and Distinguished Tradition

How was the discipline of fasting used by the Early Church to meet humanitarian needs?

How did the early monks use fasting to support missionary endeavors?

What role did fasting have during the revivals of the eighteenth and nineteenth centuries?

How do poor Christians of Mizoram, India, use fasting to support missions?

What project have you identified as the beneficiary of your fast?

## How to Observe the Widow's Fast

Read pages 105-107

The Widow's Fast can be much more meaningful if you are prepared for it. Allow your fast to minister to you as you seek to minister to others. The following questions will guide you as you prepare to observe the Widow's Fast:

What significant humanitarian needs are felt by people in your church and community?

What are ten things you enjoy regularly that others may never have?

How much of your food budget will you sacrifice during this fast?

As you pray, which need concerns you most?

What reputable agencies are working to meet that need?

For whom will you pray during your fast?

How will you identify with those in need during the fast?

How will you continue to work to meet this need?

# Practicing the Widow's Fast

What steps will you take to learn more about the people and culture that you are trying to help?

What problem are you hoping to address in the Widow's Fast? Be as specific as possible in expressing your purpose in fasting.

As you begin fasting, what will be the character of this fast? From what foods are you abstaining?

When will you begin and end this fast? How often do you intend to repeat this fast?

As you take inventory of your present lifestyle, what changes could be made to free additional resources to meet the needs of others? Which of these changes will you make first?

## A Word of Prayer

Heavenly Father,
The poor are indeed among us today. While there are many people in need, in recent days I have become particularly concerned about the suffering of ________________________________. I want to be part of Your plan to meet that need. That is why the funds I save through fasting are being sent to ____________________________ for their humanitarian work among these people. Beyond this, I want to do more. Lord, as I follow Your leading in my life and observe the Widow's Fast, open my eyes to other things that can be done to meet this need and show me what I can do to help. Please meet the need faced by these people and help me do everything I ought to see this prayer answered. In Jesus' name, I pray. Amen.

## Looking Ahead

Making decisions is a part of daily life. You made a decision when you began working through this guide to study the discipline of fasting. Some decisions you make are good. Others are not as good as you would have hoped. In the next chapter, we will consider the Saint Paul Fast and discover the role of fasting in the decision-making process. Prepare for your study by identifying significant decisions you will make during the next month, and begin asking God for His guidance as you seek to make the best decision in each situation.

CHAPTER SIX

# NOTES

# 7

# The Saint Paul Fast

A retiring bank president was once asked the secret of his success. "Two words," he responded. "Good decisions." Then he was asked the secret of making good decisions. After a moment of thought, he answered, "Two words: bad decisions." For that successful businessman, the process of learning how to make good decisions had been learned through living with the consequences of bad decisions.

Most of us would like to make better decisions. As Christians, we believe God is interested in the affairs of our lives and that His will is best. Therefore, it is important that we discern the will of God and make decisions in harmony with His will. In this study, we will consider how the Saint Paul Fast can help us make good decisions.

# How Does God Speak to Us?

Read pages 111-115

How did God use fasting in the life of Paul to redirect him?

If God were to guide you today, what are some of the means by which He is most likely to do so?

How has God given you direction in the past? How did you know He wanted you to respond to a situation in a particular way?

How important is timing in the decision-making process?

Have you ever found yourself making the right decision at the wrong time? What happened? How could things have been different?

What factors can cause us to make bad decisions?

Which of these factors is most likely to influence you to make a bad decision?

How can you avoid or minimize this factor in your decision-making process?

# FIVE STEPS TO DECISION MAKING

**READ PAGES 115-117**

Answer the following questions to help you make the difficult decision you are currently facing:

What decision do you need to make?

What have you done to avoid making this decision?

How would you describe the problem you face?

Where can you gain additional information about this situation?

Based on the available information, what are all the possible solutions to your problem?

There may not be a perfect solution. Which of the available options is the best solution to your problem?

## Prescription for the Saint Paul Fast

The following questions will help you work through the ten steps involved in gaining life-changing insight and wisdom through the Saint Paul Fast.

When during your day can you set aside time to listen to Jesus while you fast?

What questions are you asking about yourself?

How is God likely to reveal insight to you?

What are you doing that might hinder God from speaking to you?

What is your attitude before God as you begin this fast?

Have you given God permission to examine and teach you?

What are you doing about what God has already said to you?

How willing are you to wait for God's timing?

With whom are you planning to consult before making your decision?

How will you respond when others misunderstand your decision?

## Practicing the Saint Paul Fast

**Read pages 125-127**

What specific problem are you hoping to address in the Saint Paul Fast? Be as specific as possible in expressing your purpose in fasting.

As you begin fasting, what will be the character of this fast? From what foods are you abstaining?

When will you begin and end this fast? How often do you intend to repeat this fast?

What Scriptures will you be reading during your fast?

What biblical principles apply in this situation?

What creative alternatives have you considered?

Which of these alternatives is best in this situation?

Is there a way to improve upon your decision? How?

Are you confident this is the best decision available?

What steps are involved in implementing this decision?

## A Word of Prayer

Heavenly Father,

I am faced each day with decisions. Some appear minor, the kind I have no difficulty in making. Others may overwhelm me. I face a decision now about ____________________________________ and I need Your help. I need Your insight into my situation to better understand the problem. I need Your vision to see potential solutions to that problem. I also need Your wisdom and spiritual discernment to choose the best decision in my situation. Lord, as I follow Your leading in my life and observe the Saint Paul Fast, guide me through the decision-making process. Grant me the insights I need to make decisions that bring glory and honor to You. Help me as I seek to implement my decision according to the biblical principles You have revealed to me. In Jesus' name, I pray. Amen.

## Looking Ahead

We live in an era in which people are increasingly concerned about their health. As we age, we begin to experience the consequences of our unhealthy lifestyles. Some Christians who might practice the discipline of fasting hesitate to do so because of health concerns. In the next chapter, we will look more carefully at various health aspects of fasting as we study together the Daniel Fast. Prepare for your study by asking God to show you the physical consequences of fasting for you.

# NOTES

# 8

# THE DANIEL FAST

Diabetes, high blood pressure, heart disease, stroke and cancer are just a few of a growing number of health conditions common in our society today that are rare in more primitive cultures. Many doctors identify our unhealthy lifestyles as contributing to the development of these conditions. Some doctors have used fasting as part of the process for treating these conditions and have experienced some degree of success in correcting these problems.

This increasingly common medical practice is not unlike the test proposed by Daniel in Babylon. The Daniel Fast eliminates fats and cholesterol while increasing fiber. The result will be improved health. In this chapter, the Daniel Fast points out the health benefits associated with fasting.

While fasting may promote better health for many, a person with a significant medical condition should consult his or her personal physician prior to beginning a fast. A peanut butter sandwich may be viewed as an effective way to give children the fiber and proteins they need for their growing bodies, but the same meal given to someone allergic to peanuts could result in death. Specific questions about how your body might respond to a change in your diet should be discussed with your health professional.

# Fasting, Health and Healing

Why would someone enter into the Daniel Fast?

How did God use a prescribed diet to prevent the Israelites from getting diseases common among the Egyptians?

What is the purpose of the foods to be eaten during the Daniel Fast?

How can the Daniel Fast assist in the healing process?

What physical benefits does the body derive from fasting?

## THE PHYSICAL BENEFITS OF FASTING

The physical benefits associated with fasting are discussed from a different perspective in Appendix 1, excerpted from Dr. Russell's book *What the Bible Says About Healthy Living*. Dr. Russell is a medical doctor who recognizes certain health benefits associated with fasting and advocates periodic fasts for health reasons.

How does fasting help the body heal itself?

What specific medical conditions have been successfully treated with fasting, according to Dr. George Thampy?

How has fasting proved helpful in improving the mental health of some patients?

How does fasting help some people overcome food addictions?

## PRESCRIPTION FOR THE DANIEL FAST

Answering the following questions will help you prepare to observe the Daniel Fast for health and healing:

What specific problems can you identify in your present diet? What are the potential health risks associated with these problems?

How would improved health help you better serve the Lord?

What dietary changes are you implementing during this fast?

How has sin contributed to your poor health?

To whom will you be accountable during this fast?

What aspect of good health will you study during the fast?

How will you respond if there is no improvement in your health after the fast?

## Practicing the Daniel Fast

What specific problem are you hoping to address in the Daniel Fast? Be as specific as possible in expressing your purpose in fasting.

As you begin fasting, what will be the character of this fast? From what foods are you abstaining?

When will you begin and end this fast? How often do you intend to repeat this fast?

What new insights have you received as a result of your Daniel Fast?

What long-term lifestyle changes have you implemented as a direct result of your Daniel Fast?

What steps are you taking to help ensure your health remains strong for years to come?

## A Word of Prayer

Heavenly Father,
I am beginning to reap in my life the fruit sown during years of neglect and abuse of my body. Like many of my contemporaries, I would prefer to enjoy good health and a long life. But to achieve this goal, I recognize the need to repent from the way I have been treating the temple of the Holy Spirit and practice better stewardship in caring for the body You have given me. I sense the Daniel Fast may be an important part of that stewardship. Lord, as I follow Your leading in my life and observe the Daniel Fast, begin the process of healing my body and restoring my health. Make me sensitive to what You want to accomplish in my body, and accept my body as a living sacrifice to You. In Jesus' name, I pray. Amen.

## Looking Ahead

"A good name is to be chosen rather than great riches" (Proverbs 22:1). Our name and reputation is the most valuable asset most of us possess. In the next chapter, we will consider the John the Baptist Fast and how the discipline of fasting can help us establish our reputation and extend our influence. Prepare for your study by asking God to show you things in your life which may be hindering your testimony.

CHAPTER EIGHT

# NOTES

9

# The John the Baptist Fast

As the saying goes, "No matter how clean the water is, people won't drink it if it comes in dirty glasses." As true as that may be in the case of a cool cup of refreshing spring water, it is even more true in the case of those who would dispense the water of life. Many people need to see the difference the gospel has made in the lives of believers before they will give the message of the gospel the serious attention it deserves.

One of the most credible preachers of all time was the prophet who introduced Jesus to the world. From the experience of John the Baptist, we discover how fasting can be a tool God uses to expand our sphere of influence as our testimony is established. As you work through the studies in this chapter, ask God to show you how you can become "a vessel for honor, sanctified and useful for the Master, prepared for every good work" (2 Timothy 2:21).

# FASTING FOR OUR REPUTATION

What is the "double obligation" of the Christian?

How can God extend our righteousness when we have no righteousness?

How can the John the Baptist Fast affect our critics?

What criticisms do you face that may be reversed by this fast?

## Establishing a Great Testimony

The heart of fasting is sacrifice. How does this spirit of sacrifice affect the nature of our fast?

How did fasting impact the influence of John the Baptist?

How was his fast a reflection of his deeper commitment to God?

What is involved in being filled with the Holy Spirit?

What effects did fasting have on John's ministry?

How might fasting impact your reputation and ministry?

## Prescription for the John the Baptist Fast

The following questions will guide you through the steps to preparing for your own John the Baptist Fast:

How would you evaluate your present influence on others?

How would you like to influence others?

What kind of reputation do you want to have?

What commitments to Christ are you prepared to make?

What areas of your life remain outside of Christ's control?

How will this fast change your lifestyle?

Is this fast an event or process in your life?

How long do you need to observe this fast?

Are you facing a significant personal crisis? What is it?

What is the nature of the testimony you seek?

## PRACTICING THE JOHN THE BAPTIST FAST

What specific issue are you hoping to address in the John the Baptist Fast? Be as specific as possible in expressing your purpose in fasting.

As you begin fasting, what will be the character of this fast? From what foods are you abstaining?

When will you begin and end this fast? How often do you intend to repeat this fast?

Evaluate what you are about to do. Is the fast you are proposing healthy or harmful to you physically? Has it become a legalistic attempt to please God in the flesh or do you truly seek God's work in your life?

Why are you fasting in this way?

How sincere are you in your vow/decision to fast?

## A Word of Prayer

Heavenly Father,
My failure to be all You call me to be has brought disgrace to Your name and robbed You of glory. Forgive me for setting my own interests and desires above my commitment to glorify You in all I say and do. Lord, as I follow Your leading in my life and observe the John the Baptist Fast, I ask You to search me, examining every aspect of my life, and show me those areas You want to change. Grant me the grace to be receptive to Your Word and submit to the principles You want to apply in my life. In Jesus' name, I pray. Amen.

## Looking Ahead

The Scriptures use many images to describe the Christian life and ministry, including that of a battle. We are engaged in spiritual warfare against a very powerful enemy committed to hindering our progress in the Christian walk in any way he can. A spiritual battle can only be won with spiritual weapons, including the weapon of prayer and fasting. In the next chapter, we will consider the Esther Fast for spiritual protection from the evil one. Prepare for your study by asking God to make you sensitive to the spiritual forces at work in your church and community.

# NOTES

## 10

# The Esther Fast

While the disciples experienced many successes in their public ministry with Christ, on at least one occasion they encountered an individual with a spiritual problem they were unable to resolve. Recognizing the unmet need in the life of a family, Jesus stepped in to rescue the situation. He cast out a demon and restored a young boy to his right mind. Puzzled and confused, the disciples wondered why they had been unsuccessful in their attempts to do the same. Jesus responded, "This kind can come out by nothing but prayer and fasting" (Mark 9:29).

As Christians, we are engaged in spiritual warfare against an enemy that is stronger than we. But as strong as our enemy is, God is more powerful. We can experience spiritual victory when we depend upon God to fight on our behalf. One of the weapons God has given us to engage in spiritual warfare is the discipline of fasting. In this chapter, we will study the Esther Fast to discover how fasting protects us from the evil one.

# Fasting Through Many Dangers

Taking a stand for Christ can be costly. What are some of these dangers faced by Christians today? What has your faith cost you personally?

Many Christians do not believe in evil forces or demonic spirits. Why do you think many American Christians struggle with the reality that there are evil spirits at work in our world?

How does the Esther Fast differ from the rite of exorcism?

How do you feel when you read the accounts of apparent protection from the evil one described on page 160? Have you had similar experiences in your life?

How does the Esther Fast differ from the final petition of the Lord's Prayer, i.e., to "deliver us from the evil one" (Matthew 6:13)?

It has been said that although the name of God does not appear in the story of Esther, the hand of God is evident throughout. How did God protect Esther and her people from a significant threat to their peace and security?

## Prescription for the Esther Fast

There are nine steps involved in observing the Esther Fast. The following questions will guide you through your own Esther Fast:

Describe the danger you are presently facing. What is the source of this danger?

What is the nature of your personal battle?

Under God's authority, how will you respond to the enemy?

For what specific requests will you pray during this fast?

What are the possible limitations in your situation that may not be touched by the fast?

Whom have you enlisted to fast with you in this matter?

What victory strategy has God given you during your fast?

What pieces of spiritual armor are you using? Which pieces are you lacking?

How has God protected you during your fast?

## Practicing the Esther Fast

For whom do you intend to fast for spiritual protection?

How significant is the spiritual attack? Who is fasting with you in this matter?

What specific problem are you hoping to address in the Esther Fast? Be as specific as possible in expressing your purpose in fasting.

Are you willing to abstain from this fast if God makes it clear your problem is not related to spiritual warfare? What would it take to convince you God wants you to consider other possibilities?

As you begin fasting, what will be the character of this fast? From what foods are you abstaining?

When will you begin and end this fast? How often do you intend to repeat this fast?

## A Word of Prayer

Heavenly Father,
I am in a battle I cannot win alone. I not only need Your help, I need You to fight this battle for me. Intervene in those areas over which I have no control and protect me from attacks I cannot withstand. Strengthen me to endure the conflict You allow me to face, and show me Your way of escape in each situation I encounter. Watch over and protect my family and others who have engaged the enemy with me. Grant us a victory that will bring glory to You and allow for the advancement of Your agenda in the world today. Lord, as I follow Your leading in my life and observe the Esther Fast, show me the things in my life that give the enemy an advantage and hinder You from accomplishing Your purposes. Deliver me from the evil one. In Jesus' name, I pray. Amen.

CHAPTER TEN

# Notes

## II

# Choosing the Fast God Chooses for You

Together we have examined nine different approaches to fasting and considered how God can use each one to accomplish His purposes in our lives. Our study has followed the outline suggested in Isaiah 58:6-8, one of the key passages on fasting in Scripture. God chose a fast for Israel, one expressed in the nine disciplines of fasting we have been studying. Unfortunately, Israel failed to fast God's way. As a result, their fast proved to have little value and was ineffective in pleasing God.

Is it possible Christians could be guilty of the same wrong approach to fasting practiced by Israel? It is important that we fast the fast(s) God chooses for our lives. Take time now to reconsider each of the nine fasts and determine which need to be practiced on a regular basis in your life.

What is the purpose of the Disciple's Fast?

How significant is that need in your life at present?

Is this God's chosen fast for you at this time? ❑ Yes ❑ No

What is the purpose of the Ezra Fast?

How significant is that need in your life at present?

Is this God's chosen fast for you at this time? ❑ Yes ❑ No

What is the purpose of the Samuel Fast?

How significant is that need in your life at present?

Is this God's chosen fast for you at this time? ❑ Yes ❑ No

What is the purpose of the Elijah Fast?

How significant is that need in your life at present?

Is this God's chosen fast for you at this time? ❑ Yes ❑ No

What is the purpose of the Widow's Fast?

How significant is that need in your life at present?

Is this God's chosen fast for you at this time? ❑ Yes ❑ No

What is the purpose of the Saint Paul Fast?

How significant is that need in your life at present?

Is this God's chosen fast for you at this time? ❑ Yes ❑ No

What is the purpose of the Daniel Fast?

How significant is that need in your life at present?

Is this God's chosen fast for you at this time? ❑ Yes ❑ No

What is the purpose of the John the Baptist Fast?

How significant is that need in your life at present?

Is this God's chosen fast for you at this time? ❑ Yes ❑ No

What is the purpose of the Esther Fast?

How significant is that need in your life at present?

Is this God's chosen fast for you at this time? ❑ Yes ❑ No

What is/are God's chosen fast(s) for you?

## Looking Ahead

We began this series of studies on the discipline of fasting by noting that it was one of the disciplines God established to achieve spiritual breakthroughs in our lives and the lives of others about whom we care deeply. We have considered together nine different biblical fasts and how each can produce significant spiritual results in your life.

This may have been little more than an interesting study for you. As a result of this study, you now have a greater understanding of some part of Scripture.

If you observed one or more of the fasts described in this study, however, you have now experienced something of this spiritual discipline in your life, perhaps for the first time. Your fasting experiences may have resulted in spiritual victories that will be a source of encouragement to you and to others in the years to come.

Whatever your early results, my hope is that you have begun to develop a spiritual discipline that will become a growing part of your Christian walk.

CHAPTER ELEVEN

# NOTES